She Inserts the Key

To my Parents

She Inserts the Key

Marianne Burton

Seren is the book imprint of
Poetry Wales Press Ltd.
57 Nolton Street, Bridgend, Wales, CF31 3AE
www.serenbooks.com
Facebook: facebook.com/SerenBooks
Twitter: @SerenBooks

ISBN: 978-1-78172-038-7
Kindle ISBN:078-1-78172-040-0
e-book ISBN:987-1-78172-039-4

A CIP record for this title is available from the British Library.

The publisher acknowledges the financial assistance of the Welsh Books Council.

Cover art:
'Ashima – Endless, Limitless, Without Boundaries', mosaic by Laura Harris

Printed in Bembo by Berforts Group, Stevenage.

Contents

The Flowers

after Giacometti

Flowers are not fragile.

They rise again,
ripe and capricious,

they petal over cracks in concrete,
seed in the mulch of our dead.

Water or fire, grey or green,
no combination of elements
but some flower must exult in it.

If one is picked, another drinks its sun.

Their darkness is not our darkness.

The Woman Who Turned To Soap

I have lain so long in my damp ground grave
that a slow alkaline hydrolysis has transformed
my adipose tissue into luxury goods.

I am saponified, as the fattest whale
once floating unctuously in the Bering Sea.
White, sterile, and so hard. A brick.

I shall choose my own colouring,
a delicate raspberry ripple, sucrose red,
and my own perfume, from orris and anise,

prepuce of deer, beaver perinea,
secretions from the double anal pouch of cats,
and withered roses crushed in alcohol.

All my life I was dutiful. I polished, scrubbed,
I wouldn't let pets in the house, or people
until they shed their shoes, scoured their hands.

I wouldn't permit my husband in my bed
unless he showered; refused to wash his clothes
with mine, mixing his filth with my pure linen.

I smelt my body, changed my underwear,
deodorised six seven fourteen times each day,
sluiced each pore milk-sweet with chemicals.

Now I long for dissolution, fusion with the sea,
to churn with bladderwrack, foam with the waves,
to lick clean the toes of pink-footed petrels,

to spread my paste one molecule thick,
to lather the face of the welcoming waters.
Thin at last, dear God, finally thin.

Note: *The Mütter Museum in Philadelphia possesses the 'soap lady',
the body of an extremely obese woman, which is almost entirely saponified.*

Owls at Midnight

Not carol singers swinging lanterns
this time, but singing nonetheless.
Your father dropping ash, turns
from the television to the sound,

then resettles to his film. I lift you
in Barbie pyjamas, dough-warm,
and bring you to the window.
Two owls are talking to each other.

One squats on our bathroom roof,
a cottage-loaf swivelling necklessly;
the other is in the trees, the far side
of the sheep, past the silo, over the stream.

Each time the far one calls, the near one
elongates and whistles like a steam train;
then, in the answering silence, he trembles
his whole body, waiting for the female

from her wood post, before her wondering
call comes again, and he whoos with all
the bagpipe of his gut. Call, silence,
call, overlap, lose sequence, take it back.

'Look,' I say 'look'. But you are tired,
your head has slumped against my head.
Owls have no power for you, any more
than *Good King Wenceslas* last year.

I take you back to bed, grizzling
with misery, wrap you in sheets,
then wander back downstairs
to tend the drooping fire.

There are foxes in the lane, and voles
make fragile tunnels through the grass.
'I told you she wouldn't care,' he says.
The garden is silent. Something cries.

Meditations on the Hours

Midnight: Hallaton: Before the Storm

The San Andreas fault of the night.
A line of blue zeroes rises by the bedside.
Janus stands alarmed, staring four-eyed
at the quick, dead, and squatting out of sight.

Through the window the landscape creaks.
No hint of rain, though trees are shifting
foot to foot, insects have earthed, and in
the lane bats have stopped their slow ticks.

Now, in the owl-stirred blackness –
moon in the birdbath, wind in the grass –
something is getting up, filing its iron nails.

On the garden bench, a book flicks its leaves
over and back, as if being re-assessed,
as if being read by a critic not easily pleased.

1am: Lille: Night Walk with Falling Television

Street lights and little moon. Our shoes
echo on the cobbles as old Lille sleeps.
Ducks ruffle on the steps by the city pond.

From the air a television, eighties weight
and size, falls past us with straight grace
wringing the silence like Salvation brass.

Glass powder and plastic splinters rip
across our feet. The plug has been cut;
its slit cord lies among the debris innocent
as liquorice. From above, backlit, a woman
looks out, then a man. No noise, no shouting.

We are x-ray white, in as many pieces
as the punched stars, demanding narrative
where none exists, raging at the stones.

Four Village Poems from the Chinese

Shift

after Wang Wei

Halfway through the midden of our years
we bought a house in a Midlands valley.

Now when depression hits I wade with hares
through wheat, or walk in pasture with Charolais;

I stroll to the ford, then draw in the garden
under jasmine, watching the clouds roll past,

or talk about horse-ploughs to Gordon,
how the turn is always the hardest part.

Thanks for your email

after Wang Wei

You drove through Hallaton?
Do I want the news? You bet.

Outside our back bathroom,
is the greengage flowering yet?

On forgetting my keys

after Du Fu

Dodging drunks on the road, I come home at one
to a quiet house. Not even the hall light on.

The Great Bear prowls overhead. A satellite blips
its path through space grazing Cassiopeia's tips.

I call, knock, throw stones at his window. No good.
A donkey brays; our barn owl rasps in the wood.

Nothing for it but to watch the stars, and yawn
away the hours, until Mars rises with the dawn.

I know I've already said goodbye

after Du Fu

Goodbye again. Yes, I'm crying. I'm lonely
stuck here in the back of beyond, when only
yesterday we serenaded the moon, we kissed,
we hugged. We always get on when we're pissed.

It's fine for you; everybody sings your glory,
three top guys rate you. A different story
here for me: a river village white with mould,
a damp house, silence, slowly growing old.

Lacrimae Rerum

In cradles of children left to cry,
lost bottles express their spots of milk.

The swat in swinging its parabola
sprays blood over window and curtain.

The kettle spurts sorrow upwards
on the kitchen cupboard's underside

and the lavatory cistern dribbles
one drop at a time re-filling to pre-

cisely that same half-centimetre, to
exactly that familiar limescale rim.

And here in the fridge the butter block
squeezes out salty condensation

in memory of the calf who died
milk-orphaned, its lips still sucking.

Meditations on the Hours

2am: Islington: Night Feed

My blue-skinned parasite, my warm-lipped fish,
dovetailing back to being the one body
we once were, snug-fitting – the other joinder,
not lovers, but lovers, my breast, your mouth,
the suckle rhythm of the two-beat blood,
heart flow of pull and swallow,
casein and protein, sleep and serotonin.

My co-conspirator. Your meninges throb
through your fontanelle as we drift towards
the deep sea dream of the calved whale
and all the other mammals in your brother's book:
the ewe, the ox, the lemur, the manatee,
the kinkajou, kangaroo, chevrotain,
the cloud leopard, elephant shrew,

3am: The Error, Holland Park

When lovers lying in strange beds regret
the act, waking to the weight
of unfamiliar coverings, reflect
on knowledge not worth gaining.

When all the longing is to have the yearning
back, and lose the consummation.
When the other's moled shoulders turn
into a drumming dot-to-dot of skin.

Then the quiet dressing at the bedside,
finding the furthest bathroom, the slink outside,
the swift glance back at the façade,
Portland stone, Victorian pelmets.

Heels click like white sticks on the pavement,
coins jingle like pieces of silver in a hip pocket.

The Green Girl's Husband

Her country was called St. Martin's Land, and had churches.
The sun rarely rose,
but a brighter country could be seen from theirs, divided
by a broad river.

I came from King's Lynn, settled at St. Mary's of the Wolf-pits,
husband to the bean-eater,
though she was never green in my day, nor any part
or fold I ever saw.

Nathless in spring her sweat turned slippery as sap. She smelt
as a pond
when heat sets off weed,
or wheat after rain when the heads swell and dampness
forces the husks apart.

Her lips tinged with a slight blue. She looked askance
at me then
as if my stomach might turn,
but I was ever a one for dawn fowling, reed-reek,
still water slapping
the prow of my punt.

The Lux and The Lumen

in memoriam mfb

I

is what they call sickle.
Her balloon
has deflated to a sac.
She has
not eaten in three days
and was
barely there the last time I looked.

The veil
between her and the next world
is so frail
a breeze could snuff her out.
And then
where will we be at night
when
only the stars are left to us?

II

400 lux
sunrise, sunset, or a brightly-lit office
10 lux
candle at distance of one foot
1 lux
moonlight at high altitude in tropical latitudes
tenth lux
full moon on clear night
one hundredth lux
quarter moon on clear night
one thousandth lux
moonless night sky, clear
ten thousandth lux
moonless night sky, clouded
one twenty-two hundred thousandth lux
the stars and nothing else.

III

I danced under neon strips,
played in City basements,
never walked the fields at night.

The difference between
the lux and the lumen is
the second is light given,
the first is light received.

They are rarely the same.

Meditations on the Hours

4am: Kitchen Table, East Ewell

This is the hour when, dressing gown
from Debenhams, half-slippers from
the little man in the village, she comes
downstairs to make a pot of tea
and worry about our wasted lives.

I approach: note a cold sore on her lip,
count the white verticals
powdering her heels.

Mother, all our lives are wasted.
Look, my poor childish words
have already outlived you.

She does not know she is dead yet,
has entered the place where she began,
the usual unexpected human state of non-being.

5am: London: I have held conversations

on bridges, that would make you weep
with embarrassment. Declarations of love
for soft-muscled balding men who drank,
speeches of betrayal to handsome boys
who loved me ferociously, but seemed
a little safe. Meanwhile the river gleamed
and lied about its purity, its noise
lost under traffic as it hugged the dank
places, dens of tears and tight lacing, rough
sleep, soiled bodies, and the three a.m. leap.
Quiet and close it ran, Battersea, Chelsea,
Blackfriars, Southwark, waiting for the E
minor tinkle of scales falling from eyes,
flash of spit, and maiden flush of sunrise.

Winter Arriving Early

A cataract has glazed the eye
of the wine glass we abandoned
in the garden overnight.

I trace the crackling
of claret with my finger
and poke it through to the lees.

The lake itself sports a monocle,
so swans stand bent
and humbled on the grass,

and orange blocks of goldfish
race under our pond,
bathers behind frosted glass.

I heat a Le Creuset pan
and rest it on the ice
so the fish can breathe.

At the white circle's edge
their lips break the surface
mouthing grace.

The Elephant-Headed God

It was Aruna who, flush from Feng Shui
in her own home, noticed him; only his trunk
and crown showed over dishevelled
copies of *Anna Karenina* and *Madame
Bovary*, a borrowed score of *Katya*.
'There'll be trouble if you leave him there,'
she said. 'Ganesha is a jealous god.
Neglect him, he'll be after his revenge.'

It took me a month or so, like most chores,
to move him to the radiator shelf
— the one uncluttered surface in the house —
under the Erté print of *La Dame Aux
Camélias*, where he sat, deity
of our crossroads, watching the coming and
playing between living room, music room,
and bedroom. And in truth his standing there

did stir memories of lives before this one,
when all our holidays were honeymoons:
Egyptian cotton sheets in French chateaux,
a bed with a view over San Zanipolo,
chewing a late naan breakfast into
the emporium in Old Delhi where
we found him. Believing as we did then
in the immune godhead of the couple.

He looks baleful still. I must wash away
the dust that clogs his feet and the rat
crouching by his chair. His soapstone
pedestal has a crack that catches on
my skin. He'll need careful handling.
Some days as I pass I press my thumb
into his outstretched palm as a gesture
of reconciliation. We'll come through.

The Devil's Cut

Calves' feet upset me.
They have a frayed fragility,
a look of things born to be used.
Their two-toes splay across the grass
unhealed, as if a herdsman
had smashed his axe up into
the cushioned sole, severing it
from back to front, like a clog
that splits on a hard road.

Cows' foot soup and stew are made
from the feet and shins of calves,
before the hoof capsules develop
and the cow claws grow horn-hard.
Anteriors are cut at the knee joint,
posteriors at the knuckle. Pluck
after scalding, or shave, or skin.
Bone and chop for zampa burrata.
Ideal for invalids and during lactation.

It is difficult to sleep some nights
for cows calling to their calves
huddled in the top field outside
our bedroom window, tagged
for Melton market. Their feet
slipping on the lorry's ramp at 5 a.m.
I lie and listen for my daughter's tread,
padding in the dark from her bed
to mine. Veal-pink and cloven.

Meditations on the Hours

6am: University College Hospital: Maternity

There were some good moments.

OK, not pacing the corridors at 2am,
nor calling security on the two lads
shooting up in the Ladies,
nor you saying 'we're too old for this'
as I crossed over into Stage Three,

but the joy of pethidine
as needle slid into muscle
seas rolled backwards
undulations of incomprehensible
modulations of petrel porpoise torquoise turtle

before the Lark Stopped Ascending
and Simply Red started singing
'Money's Too Tight To Mention.'

7am: Mauritius: To The Sea

Your hills are more lush than any pasture,
your crop more plentiful, your grass more green.
Each morning I smell your fringe before
opening my eyes. You salt-pique my brain
and draw me out to stamp-dance on the sand.
Each blue dawn opens with my garden
pricked out with new shells, contraband
oozing fat-footed slugs, slithy and waxen.

Sea, it is time I settled with myself.
I want your stubborn pulsing to glut my
need for cradling: to sleep and be rocked.
I want to sit on a low stone shelf
imagining breakfast, and to plait my
daughter's wind-knotted hair, lock over lock.

The Singer and The Catch

It was not straight doing.
A witch told him how to hold me, to throw
his shirt over my back when I surfaced,
pulling up on the boat's side to hear him sing.
He was a small man, not much to look at,
with a black tooth and a short beard,
brown and white, the plumage of granite.
He caught me fair in my woman's shape
as I lay in the shell of the boat winded,
caught on the turn, my legs still legs.

The next night he came home from fishing,
I was sat in the kitchen, bemused by the pots,
the fire too hot, the cutlery too reminiscent
of fish hooks to keep me comfortable.
Where's my supper then? he said, *woman,*
as if to emphasise I was woman now for him,
fleshed and flayed. He hit my face, lightly,
a caress, a joke, but the intent was serious,
and the men in the doorway jeered,
and a woman laughed. One I said.

Two months later the village had a wedding.
Not ours. Still, he was singing in the evenings
and each time his voice sounded the spell held;
I couldn't move from the room it was so sweet.
The men stared at the dust on my black coat,
the woman raised her eyebrows at my clogs.
I'd never tasted wine and after a time
I spun and laughed, then wept at the sorrow
the bride would know. He slapped me hard,
weeping at a marriage. Two I said.

Shortly after, but a long time it seemed,
one of the men was trapped in the nets,
turned up bloated and green on the beach.
Not my man though. At the funeral
they poured an oily orange water which bit;
and after a glass I threw back my head
and laughed at the pain he was spared,
the dead man. A great blow he dealt me
this time to the side of my head. The eyes
of the woman danced as she watched. Three I said.

I was out of his home then in my black coat
and away that night.

But his singing would carry down to the beach.
I would crawl through the graves to peer in
where he sat in the firelight with his one candle;
fire and cat hissing at my face at the window.
The woman lay across his lap and laughed,
and he – he turned and pointed at her,
separated her long fingers, not webbed
at all, drew her skirt up above her knees
and pointed to her feet, real feet with toes,
and he opened his mouth and he sang.

I did not want his coarse beard, his bruises,
his black greasy kitchen, or the sweat of his bed,
but I wanted the music and that they knew,
as their faces hardened into spite, and I slid
from the sill, across the pebble shale, back
into the sea where the music doesn't hurt.

For A Plain Man

For a plain man you have fancy writing.
It announces itself on envelopes
in a fanfare of loops and curlicues.
Your letters clasp hands to dance galliards,
throw each other through the air, swooping
down lower than is strictly legible,
deeper than any teacher would have ticked.

You must have practised it under the desk
of the village school that wrote you off,
with short blunt pencils and scraps of paper
salvaged and stored in the empty inkwells,
working up rococo scripts whimsical
enough to summarise the man you prayed
you would become, just to spite them.

None of it comforts you of course. Not
your florid penmanship, nor the fact that
you are now important. The child still sits
under an alphabet frieze in cheap clothes,
tight-lipped, trying to coil his pot hooks into Os
of wonder and praise. You can't get back
to tell him it worked out. None of us can.

Meditations on the Hours

8am: Man Ironing, Camden

Naked, bending away from me, his back framed
between two pots of roasting herbs, rosemary
and sage, I can see neither board nor iron
from my desk, separated by two windows
and a street fussing well below our level.
But the motion of his arm is unequivocal.
He is smoothing his morning shirt, before
emerging suited and brogued for the tube.

Forward, back, the rhythm of comfortable
familiarity. As if his hand were making love
to an unseen body, idly smiling
behind the stone sill out of my eye-line,
mother-of-pearl nipples, swan-linen neck,
keeping him from work, his wife being away.

9am: The Bed, Venice

Octopus pasta on the *Stendhal* sleeper
comes briny with body sacs, like finger
ends of rubber gloves. Not one tentacle.

The whole journey's been a disappointment,
grinding sleepless over border points
in short single bunks, sulky with sweat.

But, at the Luna Hotel, the bedroom window
uncurtains to a silver screen. We view the lagoon
Prosecco-doped, lobster-soothed, stacked on pillows,
and doze across the hot Byronic afternoon.

In the morning, the city wakes slightly
hazy, wearing just the ripples in the water,
and San Giorgio Maggiore,
a single pearl earring, drips from her ear.

Changing The Sheets

Nothing more intimate
than this tending.
Though these are not
special, not wedding

sheets, no child
was born in them.
They have no rolled
hand-sewn hems,

are not embroidered
with rose or gorse.
Not new, not ironed.
Just creased, coarse,

cheap store cotton
for the night tomb
where we clutch, twins
in our feathered womb.

Not perfumed, not linen.
Just your night sweat,
acid and a peck of salt,
safe in my keeping.

Sparrowhawk

As we came from the back door, an arrow
– of thrush, or blackbird, or bullfinch – shot

from quince tree to thorn bush, tight-trailing,
as a child's kite draws its paper tail, a hawk,

which slammed, clawed feet first, into the spikes,
while lunch wriggled through a hole to freedom.

For fifteen seconds it lay crucified –
wings museum-fixed, spread-eagled by thorns –

as we watched our exhibit twist against
its pivot, its spine pull against the pinioning,

eyes extruding, beak gaping, tongue protruding,
barred feathers pinned wide for our inspection.

Then, sucking back like a tide, it unstuck, flew
straight as a catapult's slug, sharp past the gate,

leaving us piecing together what we'd seen
with what we would claim later we had seen.

Pissarro's Orchards

Fruit trees are beauty in themselves. I shall ban
anacondas seducing Eve, slithering over her lap
pleading for her to take a bite. I shall veto gang
rapes of nymphs by satyrs; will have no gods or
angels. No feather-hatted naked madam,
son complaining as he is stung by nectar-
inebriated bees; no impudent kitten, its paw
pawing its mother; no Susanna ogled by an elder.
Berry, leaf, blossom are enough. Perhaps a woman
gossiping as she strings pea trellises, an old man
daring to stoop and hoe, a haymaking group,
each worker committed to a common plan,
– taint, rot and worm avoided – one hope,
ardent and plain. Harvest is sufficient passion.

Note: *This sonnet considers Camille Pissarro's philosophy
of fit subjects for art. It includes the names of fruits broken
between the beginning and end of lines.*

Meditations on the Hours

10am: Hallaton: Oranges

Thick damp, more dense than steam, a sweat
nectared with cane, clings to the kitchen walls
as if sugar water seeped through the plaster.
Labels on the extractor fan begin to unseal
in the haze from the preserving pan's wet
turmoil of pip and rind, from the rise and fall
of muslin bags, as the crust foams faster,
and the house squeaks with the stink of peel.

And that's February. Marmalade sealed
in the pantry, while our lacklustre
complexions hold out for March. In Sevilla
oranges hang in the streets, like Marvell's
lamps in a green night. Why does no one steal
them? *We have so many*, the driver says.

11am: Hallaton: Burial of the Dead

With a sharp spade, we cut the turf
beneath the apple tree. Minus two degrees,
but the ground so mossy and damp
it scuffs up easily, and the box
(Doublebase facial wash)
sinks down as if made for the job.

Goodbye Hyacinth, she says.
Which is all anybody ever says
to the dead. As with newborns,
eloquence fails. On the other side
of the path in spring there will
be hyacinths; and there is holly,
for when the next one dies,
waiting, tight to the wall.

Fieldfare

The first hard frost froze
our breathing overnight

to patterns on the pane.
I rubbed my fingers on

the icy fishbone-feathers,
then banged a fist

until the casement gave.
White fields. White trees.

And under our window
one dead fieldfare,

exhausted after its night
flight from Sweden,

the discarded fletching
of its own arrow,

and a firethorn arching its berries
over the body, extravagant

as the Christmas feast
behind the match-girl's wall.

Viewing at the National

We have stood a full ten minutes gazing at St. Lucy,
her eyes heavy-lidded on a plate like two sad oysters,

then walk into the next room where the attendant
looks you up and down, then starts to stroll behind us

wanting you under some restraint, on a ribbon
maybe, like Uccello's dragon. Whatever happens

it won't be on his patch. A lecturer glances, stiffens,
parades his tourists to a distance, as if you might

ignite or run amok, as if whatever foreign field
or training camp I found you in had set you ticking.

You are too dark for comfort, too broad, too much
the long-pelted bull, your shoulders boxed to hide

your neck, your walk a swing of supposed
violence under your East End coat, as we pass

between massacres, torture, beheadings,
flayings, tearing by beasts, until in the cold air

we breathe out under the portico. *Not my cup of tea
really*, you say, and lay a finger lightly on my arm.

The River Flowing Under The Bank
of England Dreams of Power

Our slow-green hair has grown. Samson sings
in the loosening links of his brick chain

ancient tunes of sewage, wave, and drains.
We abrade the runs they lace us through,

we swell, we pound; soon otters, willow,
dace and cress below the human landscape

shall burst into their money rooms and break
their fishbone combs, their bead-pearl cufflinks,

coins duller than carp scales, empty wells of ink.
Bonds shall be broken, mussels prise the pyx.

Fish shall dine on floating boards, and silver-fixing
conclaves shall be lunch for oyster and clam.

City pavements tremble over our premature tomb;
the sky empowers us, we fatten, wax, grow bold.

We shall reclaim vaults, gild our snails with gold,
slew filth through their halls. We shall share nothing.

Meditations on the Hours

Noon: Liverpool Street: The Bank of Desks

A slow start these cold-blooded mornings:
we slump at our posts, avoid small movements,
stoke up on coffee while the screens focus
and we try to remember how to think.

Then, symbiosis clicking in, we weave our line,
leaf-cutters, advancing files and slices of paper,
until by noon we have reached Man Zenith,
Masters of Many Destinies, Hot-Rocking Millions.

By 2 o'clock evolution is in decline.
By 3:30 we resemble the sloth.
By 6pm are fast approaching the Andante Tree,
which moves a few centimetres a decade
(more during drought) as it delicately
picks up and replants its roots.

1pm: Castle Rising: Picnic

If there are ghosts here, they are quiet ones.

I feel nothing restless echoing in these stones
or under the grass where we sit, uncork,
parcel out foils for lunch.

The sky is fisher blue, lightening a little to the south.
Along the high ridge children run
catching at wings.
Tourists nap in the sunshine.
Leaves rub their brown paper bag percussion
and on the label of The Society's White Burgundy
a fish is leaping.

Only when I run my finger down the stone slit
where the drawbridge used to fall does something stir,
as if a grating opened in another place.

On Envying Exile

How I long for somewhere to go back to
when my strife is over, when I've made my pile,
with old folks stretching out worn rugs
saying how *verligte* I've grown, how svelte.

How I long for a language half-forgotten,
two or three passports with different faces,
an ancient music that after a few too many
makes verses weep and drums appear symbolic.

Pity the suburban born who have no
ancestral bodies buried under the porch,
no columbaria glowing with lapis frescoes,
no cemetery neglected behind the yews

where spotted stones, yellow and black,
chant names from family daguerreotypes,
where rampant roses and grass run wild
in their triumph of the root over the foot.

Pity the fringe dwellers, escaping from nowhere,
who no one could be bothered to shut in;
the un-landlocked, without hope of return,
without nostalgia. Self flowers in named places.

On damp nights I stare at sultry pools
lurking under street lamps, and I dream:
if I stood on a corner long enough
– the right corner, there are so many –

someone might say *I know your country*.
Then, no matter how cheap his offer,
I would follow the slick-talking cheat
into the shadows, knowing it wasn't so.

Three Songs of the Inarticulate

Song of the Dodo

Mare aux Songes

doo-doo doo-doo
doo-doo doo-doo

fish fruit stone
fruit fish stone
stone fruit fish
fish stone fruit
fruit stone fish
stone fish fruit

fruit fruit fruit

doo-doo doo-doo
doo-doo
doo
doo

Song of the William Morris Wallpaper

black bird black bird black bird
drib kcalb drib kcalb drib kcalb

open beak   closed beak
closed beak   open beak

       f o l
         i
      a g e

bird berry straw berry bird

black bird black bird black bird

Song for Michael who has no speech (or movement)

Mmm
Mmm
Mmm (*hungry*)
Mmm (*angry*)
Mmm (*crying*)
Mmm (*because you are
in bed and the curtain
hanging in the bar of
light from the landing
resembles a man in a
rain coat with a fedora
pulled over his eyes and
moves — hardly percepti-
bly — every few
minutes*).

dragonfly

the smallest sounds:

> a snail rasping cells
> from an ivy leaf,
> sparrows' claws
> in a broken wall;
>
> the dragonfly's clasp
> as it swings
> over the lawn,
> clicking like a trap:
>
> *look at me who*
> *threw nothing away.*
> *If your song survives*
> *a fraction of my time,*
> *if your species lives as long,*
>
> *then*

The Persistence of Vision

It is as if our eyelids had been cut off.
Light reflecting from the whitewashed church
outside the hotel room, sears our retinas.

Each Easter day dawns hot as August,
lemons bleaching to ripeness as we watch.
Blossom dies in the orchards, buds wilt,

boutiques are cleared of summer stock.
We clap tight our shutters to shake out
shorts and gaudy T-shirts in the shade.

Each late morning we saunter to the beach
in swimsuits, while mass celebrants
pass us like crows, shrouded in mantillas.

Each late evening we cruise to restaurants,
while bells ring and black-hooded men
process religious statues through the streets.

This last afternoon the light is so intense
I want to set it down as memory, to sketch
you curled on the bed, naked as a faun,

as St. Sebastian. The bells toll deeper.
I varnish my nails until they flutter in
a blood-red rosary. The light still shines

and when I shut my eyes, the window brace
burns behind my lids in the shape of a cross
for a long moment. Before it fades away.

Meditations on the Hours

2pm: Summer Crossing, Iona

You should come here in winter, through rough water:
step out of a small boat, the taste of unclean salt
fouling your lips, re-firm your feet, loosen ties
of anorak and hood, and find yourself again
dishevelled, shaking, your city skin shucked off.

You should come here in winter. Not high season
for local lobster and miniature bottles
of Jack Rabbit Californian Chardonnay,
swallows nesting in the roof of Oban's Chapel,
tourists netting crabs and tanning on the beach.

If it is worth the journey, worth the prayer,
then it is worth the sickness and the damp,
the coracle's centrifuge and worry of drowning.
You should come here in winter, in rough weather.

3pm: The Ninth Hour, Calvary

By love we getten and holden.
Love shining like the scales of a herring.

By love may we be geten and holden.
Love shining like the tines of a fork.

Only by love may he be getyn & holden.
Love shining like spilt milk from a breast.

Only by love may we be getyn & holden.
Love shining like bone breaching skin.

For those who sit at the foot of a cross.
For those who suffer in the dark.

For those who have marked in their diary
the hour when, for them, a heart stopped.

The Extinction of Mary Smith Jones

last speaker of Eyak 1918-2008

Bella Coola killer whale, two Haida bears,
Gagiixiid with fish bones lodged in his lips,
Tsimshian salmon and two survivors of the flood.

In the glass front of the museum cabinet
over masks of dead and dying civilizations
push the fat reflections of the living.

Fruit of the Loom T-shirt, butterfly tattoo,
boy with MP3 player stuck in his ears,
two survivors of the push and shove.

Mary Smith Jones, last full-blooded member
of the saltwater Eyak, people of the southern flats,
dwellers of the Copper River (food-rich

with runs of chinook, coho, sockeye salmon,
only known home of the dune-dwelling sandpiper,
last nesting site of the dusky goose) has died.

And with her, the language of her nation.
Tongue-tied after her sister died, Eyak
was kept for God and for her dreams,

and for dough-faced men with microphones
who sucked her fricatives and affricates
into their dictionaries of linguistic extinction.

Grieve for the passing of Eyak; grieve
as for the passing of a skilful lover, leaving
endearments peeled and raw in a new mouth.

Grieve for Mary, Udach' Kuqax'a'a'ch',
as the past strangles in the present's grip,
as the stories die and the songs cease singing.

Bella Coola killer whale, two Haida bears,
Gagiixiid with fish bones lodged in his lips,
Tsimshian salmon and two survivors of the flood.

The Anagram Kid

This salesgirl scum serves us the garlic mussels
then refuses my debit card, claiming it's bad credit.
A shoplifter has to pilfer, so I sneaked the pepper pot
and we headed off for the tense charm of Manchester.
Some used car raced us on the motorway and won.
The truth is, it hurts being poor. The billboard said
Elvis Lives, but we don't, not so you'd notice.
You can tell I'm bored, emotionally curbed;
when you've no income, no one says, come on in.
Voices rant on, the conversation always about money.
It said 'Christine' on her name badge, on her nice shirt.
Circumstantial evidence can ruin a selected victim.
It was desperation, I said. A rope ends it. Pass me one.
A funeral is about the only real fun I can afford.
Nine thumps. A bit of punishment. She deserved it.
Listen. I didn't mean to hurt her. I'll remain silent.

A Green Oak By The Sea

in memoriam jab

In the good old-fashioned manner
of the theatre of Grand Guignol
my father laughed as he swayed

over patients in his dentist's chair,
his inquisitive drill whining
for fillings and the stench of rot.

Once he found a tomato seed
sprouting in the tartar-rich oasis
of a molar cavity, trying for roots:

while I waited in the dim recess
of reception, for Ben his dental technician
to mend my neck cross, I imagined

that man dead, tendrils gushing
from his mouth, jostling in his coffin,
pushing off the lid to sniff for air,

spiralling round a brass plate (similar
to my father's on the post outside,
'and also at 1 Harley Street'),

emerging as a tree from the manure
of the body, a tree spilling red fruit
like the green oak in the folk songs

his nurse sang me from the Russian
a chain of bright gold was round it
a chain of bright gold was round it.

Old Names

Now he has lost the hours
and days, he croons for me
songs simultaneously
charming and crude
as common words
for hedgerow flowers.

I hold his hand and scan
trains outside the window
running empty to depot.
Love-in-idleness.
Love-in-a-mist.
Love-lies-bleeding.

Meditations on the Hours

4pm: Slim Shady in Hallaton Churchyard

Flocks of winter thrushes in a field startle
like children; robin and coal tit rattle
in the bare-ribbed hedge and scramble away.
I am the solitary walker, for whom weak sun
on snow has left pavements and lane down
to the grave-yard murderous with ice.

There is a communality about people
in this bone alley. All access is equal.
No child or lover can have more of them
than I do now, who, alone in God's Acre,
watch their stones two days before New Year,
while *Stan* steals from a parked car – solemn
as any music creeping across a cathedral
close at dusk at the sealing of December.

5pm: Stoneleigh: The Lie of the Pool

I have been disillusioned since the age of ten.
My mother was an artist. She saw things differently.
When I came in from swimming she would often
ask what the water looked like, was the sea
angry or pleased? I always turned away.
I never could be bothered to humour her.
It was the school pool, mother, I would say,
ugly, noisy, with heel plasters in the water.

But she, rinsing out my costume,
saw the barnacled undersides of whales,
quickslip of dolphins, flumes
of canoes, hammocking sails,

and she would paint them for me
on her canvases, in thick oils, badly.

Encyclopaedia

I crouched over its leaves
in the perpetual gloom
of the Hoover cupboard.

It felt animal,
the raw-rubbed nap
of window leather,

and smelt vegetable,
the stink of attic boxes,
damp, and unburied bulbs.

I unfolded its back pages,
flapped diagrams
of dissected yew and apple,

the needled reservoir
beneath the bee's fur,
the frog's kinked lariat of gut,

the female torso, sawn-off
at the thighs, with pink
balloon and long-armed claws

– one left one right –
coming at you bear-like
for a treacherous hug,

and the male figure,
smooth between his legs
as a shop mannequin, who

undressed three times to show
(i) the fuchsia muscles
of a Marvel comic hero,

(ii) a tangle of blue and red
knitting wool, and (iii) the yellow
grinning man who beckoned,

while outside the window
in the summer heat
the street sent up

hooves and the cry
she said took people away,
Rag Unbone, Rag Unbone.

Sum of Our Parts

Whenever I see a pasta picture
collaged by a primary child

I see my body, contrived
from spirals and curls.

Now look, on the school-run
home, how pieces break away:

here a dog noses one aside,
here a piece breaks under a shoe.

Meditations on the Hours

6pm: Coin Du Quai Voltaire: Last Orders

We are in the slipstream of six o'clock.
Late sun slides down the side street
and everything that this morning was bright
is in shadow, everything is bone that was quick.

We are in the negative of ten o'clock.
A tree with sloughed bark picks up white,
while on the other side of the street
cathedral and confiserie put on dusk.

It is growing autumnal, but still warm
as we hunch over our last coffee pre-dinner,
hands sleeved, watch the developing film
of evening scour each table, strip off coverings.
Two men kiss with last light behind them.
A woman powders her cheeks. Dust thins.

7pm: The Mound Field, North End

At noon this field is full of larks, but not now.
Harvest is almost finished
and autumn coming on like fat Falstaff.

Many evenings I have sat and watched
our resident hare's punctual arrival;
many evenings my eyes have followed
her ear tips running from the far gate,
appearing and disappearing
between each ridge and furrow.

And one time, as I sat weeping
on this same stile, a horse came
and laid its head in my lap

as if it were not what it was

as if I were not what I am.

The Woman Who Fitted In The Sydney Opera House

Earlier this evening she sprayed on perfume,
clasped a favourite neck-chain round her throat;

there would have been a mirror to check
her outfit was presentable from all angles.

Everyone is stoical. Nobody cranes impatiently
from the balcony. No announcements are made.

Ushers smile, the conductor stands motionless
on his podium, the cellists hold their bows.

Emotion waits behind the lowered curtain
in greasepaint and *fin de siècle* costumes.

This is not that same high-water tragedy,
merely a moment of pity and embarrassment.

Still, for her, a previous existence ends here.
All goings out and comings in have altered

between Café Momus and the snow of Act Three.
All further nights will be counted from this.

The perfume will speak of it, and the chain,
and the peacock dress with appliquéd feathers

held firmly under the armpits by two strong
ambulance men while her husband walks behind.

Wren Spilling Into Water

Tail bragged with singing,
he is visible twice: as himself
and as his twin in a loose rivulet
which has escaped the stream
and threaded its way through the field.

His image flickers on the water
so it seems to shift with his energy,
as if he were wind, or a fish,
as if he had the sailor's gift
of troubling two elements at once

Behind The Cellar Door

What is going on, Mummy, behind the cellar door?

There is a party going on, children.
Hear that crazy jazz percussion,
skip of syncopation, slow drumming heavy
as the blows of Murdoch the butcher
beating his cleaver on the wooden block.
They come and go at night, children,
instruments in cases, dressed in black,
that is why we never see anybody.

What is going on, Daddy, behind the cellar door?

There is a meeting going on, children.
Poets, philosophers, politicos:
all those thinkers hitting their fists
on the table and drinking, drinking,
how they need beer to ease their thoughts.
They come and go at night, children,
books in rucksacks, dressed in black,
that is why we never see anybody.

What is going on, Uncle, behind the cellar door?

They are digging you a playroom, children.
Blades of shovels turn the stones,
pick away and pit the limestone floor.
All hours gravel slides into barrows,
pitch pine planks are nailed across the walls.
The diggers stay till dawn, children,
tools in zip bags, dressed in black.
One of us will take you down there soon.

Meditations on the Hours

8pm: Hunstanton: The Baby

That summer my mother finally had the baby,
we took a house on the Norfolk coast.
My mother wasn't well, nor the baby,
and my sister watched over me.

She measured high tide from breakwaters,
dipping me in. She timed my running
to the shops for Tizer and *Jackie*. Faster,
they'll see you're away. Say the bruises
came from slipping off the bunk. Say say.

Her game in the dark. Our car's crashed,
what body part is this? Peeled grapes,
celery, shoe horn, bath sponge, twiglets.
I dreamt I showed the pieces to my mother.
I'm so sorry, I said. So desperately sorry.

9pm: America: I have travelled on
long distance buses

I have travelled on long distance buses
rucksack for a pillow, sorbitol gum
the sole food caulking my shallow pocket.
I have fidgeted sleep between two seats,
men liqui-coughing, children pleading
'mom mom, why can't we go home to Dada?',
drivers keeping shouting on back 'Hey you,
where d'ya say ya cam from? Was it London?
Don't ya love them Sherlock Holmes movies?'

Those were bad times. Nights my imagination
screened only rapes; dozing half-flat half-flexed,
hands hawk-clawed around my purse, shrunk
and irked to an oyster's quivering sensibility,
fast cars passing on the other side, lights shining
like questions into my future. Such as it was.

The War Road

I watched the dead ride past,
horses fleeced with sweat,
foam thrown from their bits.

I heard the jingle
of bones against saddlery.
Do not forget I cried

the night we dined outside –
raspberries, quinces,
little gasps of rapture.

I heard their skeletal structures
shudder the cattle grids.
Silence ran at their heels.

Head on a Desert Road

I did not know
there were sites like this,
to be stumbled across
on a simple search.

It sits propped like a bollard
by the unmade roadside,
its dark hair
neatly trimmed,

a triangle of skin
stripped off its neck,
sinew protruding
in rags of sea wrack.

Why did you come to the desert?
What did you come to see?
A broken reed? Part-boy,
part-man. Men in khaki.

Every jeep raises a sand storm
to powder his cheeks.
From the chin down
it is only meat

and there are dogs on the road.
Still the head is whole,
the charge blew it free
like a stopper from a bottle.

Better his mother were blind
than to see him so trimmed.
Better his mother were dead.
Its hair so neatly trimmed.

Eyes half-lidded in ecstasy,
as boys listen to music.
Ecce ecce Agnus Dei.
Mouth open, as if to speak,

as if Salome herself,
letting her garment slip,
lowered a breast
to graze his blackened lips.

Chapel of Nine Altars

wood
for the new-wed
the enchanted

stone
for the lonely
the supplanted

bone
for the new-born
the uninitiated

bronze
for the fallen sons
the unappreciated

gold
for the bold
the fearless

brick
for the sick
the cheerless

tin
for the sinner
the tearless

clay
for the slayer
the unlovable

lead
for the dead
the irrecoverable

The Child Reading

The fact that we were once tree-dwelling
is apparent from her posture on the sofa.
Her arms are loose, her head relaxed as she scans
her lines frowning; but for concentration
this tight the feet must be safe, not left
dangling to attract attention from below.

I have seen lemurs in trees forks sleeping
in the same configuration, twins sometimes,
fur-fruit huddled in leaves while the deluge
steamed, as we levelled our binoculars
and wished the rain would stop so some animal
might stretch and move. And the mud, the mud.

But she is dry, this side of the window,
legs drawn in, tucked up semi-foetally.
And at the last she stretches full out, supine
in watery sun. The book has told her
sometimes a child grows undamaged, a man
lives without fear, a hope does not entirely fade.

Meditations on the Hours

10pm: Sunset and Full Moon: Brancaster Staithe and Whitby

At 10:15 in May there is still a line of red
on the horizon echoed in the marsh:
a knife gash slowly mending,
the double slash of parted lips.

I accompany myself down the coastal path
and by the time I reach the cemetery
of Deepdene Barnet – it's dark now
and deserted – the wound has healed.

When I phone you, standing on the mud jetty,
hundreds of bead crabs dead in the weed,
you say in Whitby your moon is full too.

The moon on my sea splits into the slats
of a Venetian blind, shivers into shaken ribbons,
reassembles. Penny for our thoughts.

11pm: Coffee: Cathles Road

when rich incantatory names hang in the air
like opening charms from *One Thousand And One
Nights* – Longberry, Brown Java, Blue Mountain,
Arabica, Bourbon, Monsoon Malabar –

places where, given the right inamorato, you might go –
Papua New Guinea, Ecuador,
Guatemala, Sumatra, El Salvador,
Costa Rica, Mexico, Brazil;

when half-offers hang on the tongue –
langues de chat, Bath Olivers, honey cakes,
semi-skimmed, full cream – and nobody makes
a move in case one of you has it wrong –
muscovado, soft brown, demerara –

and the music has never sounded sweeter.

The Emperor and The Nightingale

She inserts the key in the bird. He counts
her wrist turns, silently. Forty-nine, fifty.
The head picks up, the throat stretches,
the beak flicks open to reveal a pink velvet
mouth, frail and secret as a foetus's ear.
Open, pulse, close, open, pulse, close.

In the end he can't make love without it,
its repetitive metal singing, the clicking
into place of tiny strips of gold. The ritual
beginning even before entering the chamber,
as he sends ahead his favourite (stolen
from the palace of her deceased father)

to confirm the sword-smith, still sweating
from forging ornamental blades in his shop,
has stripped the machinery, re-embedded
the loose jewels, and oiled its interstices
with a mole-skin bud or owl's underfeather.
Then, flowers, towels and water replenished,

while outside hunters bring back carcases
and women bring back brine in yoked buckets,
the bird's eyes, one citrine, one diamond,
sun and moon, reflect the bed like two halves
of a fruit, each caged repetitive movement,
as she starts at the feet, kissing upwards.

Meditations on the Hours

Midnight: Darsham: Laying Down The Day

Before the light goes out, one must give thanks
for the day (so my gestalt therapist tells me).

So: for a hot Sunday; a tight-haired terrier;
a bench under trees where a one-legged cock
hopped beside his hen; a story of how Eliot
at a party once said to her sister, let us sit
under this table (very like this one) with long
linen cloths to hide them, everyone else being drunk,
and they did for two hours, saying hardly anything,
(nothing happened, her sister claimed afterwards);

What Maisie Knew; Framlingham Castle; London Pride;
Ireland's *Fantasy*; one ripe fig; three dead rabbits;
two thousand and one Chateau Cantemerle;
a little love and much liking. That's about it.

Four Water Quatrains for Primo Levi

Warum? I asked him in my poor German.
Hier ist kein warum he replied.

i.

there are no whys here
we are sixty per cent water
our bodies
ebb and fail

ii.

we are from the womb
Ptolemaic
our little world is bounded
by a sea

iii.

and after the drop
when the body is cut down
a muddy puddle
on the floor

iv.

Bring me a drink
any liquid
it is the bringing
that matters

Acknowledgements

Acknowledgements are due to the editors of the following where these poems, or versions of them, have previously appeared: *Agenda, Borderlands: Texas Poetry Review, Dark Horse, Magma, Mslexia, New Contrast, New Plains Review, New Welsh Review, Orbis, Poetry Daily, Poetry Ireland Review, Poetry London, Poetry Wales, Rialto, Salzburg Poetry Review, Shearsman, Smiths Knoll, Stand,* the *Times Literary Supplement,* Radio Four's *Poetry Please,* and in the pamphlet *The Devil's Cut* (Smiths Knoll), which was a Poetry Book Society Pamphlet Choice.

'For A Plain Man' won first prize in the Mslexia poetry competition 2006. 'Head On A Desert Road' won second prize in the *Times Literary Supplement* poetry competition 2010. 'The Emperor and The Nightingale' won third prize in the Edwin Morgan poetry competition 2010.' 'Owls at Midnight' was runner-up in the 2009 Cardiff International Poetry Competition. 'Sum of Our Parts' was one of the winners of the Parallel Universe science poetry competition 2010 organised by the Radcliffe Science Library Oxford and Kellogg College Creative Writing Centre.

I owe thanks to a lot of people, but especially to my publishers, Joanna Cutts and Michael Laskey of Smiths Knoll, and Amy Wack of Seren.